DATE DUE

Causeway

Elaine Sexton

New Issues Poetry & Prose

A Green Rose Book

New Issues Poetry & Prose
The College of Arts and Sciences
Western Michigan University
Kalamazoo, Michigan 49008

First Edition, 2008.

ISBN-10   1-930974-77-9 (paperbound)
ISBN-13   978-1-930974-77-7 (paperbound)

Library of Congress Cataloging-in-Publication Data:
Sexton, Elaine
Causeway/Elaine Sexton
Library of Congress Control Number: 2007939654

Editor   William Olsen
Managing Editor   Marianne Swierenga
Copy Editor   Natalie Giarratano
Designer   Christine Emmer
Art Director   Tricia Hennessy
Production Manager   Paul Sizer
                                The Design Center, Frostic School of A
                                College of Fine Arts
                                Western Michigan University
Printing   Cushing-Malloy, Inc.

Causeway

Elaine Sexton

New Issues

WESTERN MICHIGAN UNIVERSITY

Also by Elaine Sexton

Sleuth

for Robin

Contents

IV.

I.

Turnstile

I carry the prints of a hundred thousand
strangers in my hands, their palms
on the turnstile this morning like mine
touching the kiosk buttons, fingering
coins to pay for the *Times*. At Union Square
Station, the stale breath of others
inhabits the boxcar air. The scent of lilacs
shuttles with us from the garden to work
with our spring colds, our smokers' coughs,
the *Daily News* the others left behind
on their seats, vacant, invisible debris,
tubercular, airborne like grief, theirs
not like mine, not like anyone else's.

Lower Manhattan Pantoum

Always a bad sign
people on the sidewalk looking up.
A crowd forms, cars slow
then stop,

people on the sidewalk looking up.
I step into the pool of them
then stop.
I gape like the others.

I step into the pool of them,
become the pool
and gape like the others.
Mothers, peddlers, suits

become the pool
of a wreck.
Mothers, peddlers, suits,
my super, my neighbors,

a wreck
unfolding, undone.
My super, my neighbors,
no one is not stunned.

Unfolding, undone,
we look at our watches,
stunned.
Someone says *let's pray.*

We examine our watches.
A crowd forms. Cars stop.
Someone says *let's pray*—
always a bad sign.

Masonry

Brick of my mother's
Pittsburgh, her
weather steel-mill gray
every day, brick
of my father's Boston
law school at night,

the Federal brick
of Portsmouth, New Hampshire,
where I pined for a boy
at a brick ferry landing
and flirted
with sailors and prayer

but gave up
every brick
of every seaside city
I lived in,
so nearly the same:
Newport, New-

buryport. The whole
Eastern Seaboard's
worn bricks
crumbled alike
in the sun. Urban brick,
in particular,

the brick shelters
of love. New York
City brick, best of all,
the West Village brick,
more precisely,
where I bricked up

one life and tore it down,
one love, then
another, no more

stable. Or just as stable.
One brick at a time.
Brick of desire,

brick of loyalty, brick
of empathy, brick of guilt,
of solitude,
brick by irregular
brick.

Night. Fire

When we looked up after hours of staring
at a crimp in a log, the shooting blue
flames, puffs of smoke,
the tide that was right here had gone
way out, so the waves were now strokes of gray
in the distance, and the dark night closed in
on us, everywhere at once.

Everywhere at once the sky was touchable,
for of course it was right here, over us,
as well as way out over the smaller and smaller waves,
coming forward but still going out.

Coming forward but still going out, leaving
us to watch this crashing in and in
yet each time receding, the way our conversation
happened along those same lines.

Along those lines we managed a few
untouchable subjects, the way we imagine
we can touch a star or the moon on a night like this
but know we really can't. We imagine we see
everything more clearly, but that doesn't work
with the past. Which is what we were dealing with—
in the way families try to deal with this sort of thing.

Families deal with this sort of thing
poorly, so far as I can tell, and so when the bon-
fire loosened its hold and we stretched our mysteries out
over the sand, the way we'd never do over a meal
in one or the other's house, we heard
the lips of one wave touch another as if each spoke for us.
And words came slowly, or didn't come at all.

Slowly, or sometimes not at all, seemed better
than never. And never seemed to be coming
forward like the sky, which is always so close
and receding at the same time.

Estuary English

A sea-mark exposed my limits.
This is where loss first
opened its mouth, where
my alongshore navigation
began. I was practically born
in a tide pool, the wrack
of my family, a view
best seen in words, buried
like a razor-necked clam, my shell,
part of some bigger mystery,
solid enough to call home but not
too hard to crack. In the beak
of a gull, the earth finally showed
its shape. One minute
I swam in the sand, the next, wings
beat over my head; the sweep
of the coast showed below, lineated
as I never imagined. I hung
in the firm grip of two claws, fear
and desire. I did nothing but let them
hold me. I struggled little
once I caught sight of waves cresting
and crashing. It made no sense,
given the gravity of granite,
not to look, and keep looking.

Onion Field

Our friends wanted us to taste everything:
their dust and sweet air, their mangy
Mexican dogs, banana leaves floating,
botanical, architectural. Here, they trade
mostly roses, fields and fields of their bodies
for sale in red bundles like firewood
on the road. Here, where the barb
in the barbed wire fence
caught me, onions roasted on a grill
with clusters of chilies I never dared touch
with my tongue. Only a small thread of me
kept snagging and unraveling as crops turned,
and miles and miles of fence
framed beauty like something lit by a match.
Did I know, even then,
our friend and driver, our host,
would die, months later? And you,
whom I love, I would leave.
And the house where we stayed, year after year,
down a lane cut through onion fields,
would be sold. That I'd actually risk
not coming back to this place. Again. And again.

Denizen

I drive by this part of the island
where dead cars marry beach
grass and washtub handles
wring rust. Old dogs dream
in the dirt. And the knock
of a ball on a stick still lobbies
the dark. A streetlight sputters
thoughts, Bermuda shorts loose
on my thighs, a pale straw bag
on the seat. I cover my camera.
Here is a window I'd never
seal shut, a shade, half-drawn,
a white pull, a silent O
still swinging. Here, something torn
keeps tearing, the climate so lush
I could sip it without sugar
or crush it and smear it
for rouge. I could dress a wound
or garnish a dress with this
garish extravagance. Tell me, again,
why I'm here, stirring a taste
for the vacant, searching for home
in a thrift shop find, something a mother,
not yours or mine, left behind.

A Bird in the House

1.

The knocking and knocking
in her washing machine
brought things sharply into focus
when I raised the lid and saw her daily laundry:
a single bra, its metal clasp
hitting the walls of her white Kenmore
over and over. I said, *mother, there's nearly
nothing in here.* She busied herself at the sink
full of dishes unwashed for a week.

Shopping for bras that afternoon,
I joined her in the dressing room.
She couldn't remember her size.
Not being a mother, I saw how I'd never know
the coming-of-age of a daughter, but,
instead, I'd be a daughter helping my mother
measure this gentle harness,
the first of many stays
we'd share and let go as she needed me.

2.

Late one night my mother called my brother:
a bird in her house and she couldn't get it out,
even with her broom. He raced the dark mile
over the causeway and found no bird,
though together they thumped through every room.

She swore *there is a bird, there is a bird in the house,*
and the bird in her house was something
we whispered between us all week.

Mother, there is no bird, we said.

There is a bird, she said, *there is a bird,*
the first of many repetitions.

Maybe you know how this goes.

We turned back the clocks,
and the days turned mysteriously cold
along with the light. Her house, full of shadows,
showed how fear might draw a bird in the house.

I decided to visit more often.

A week later, alone with my mother,
I snapped on her light in the hall. An enormous
black bird knocked its frantic wings on the walls,
clawing the air over our heads.

I opened the heavy front door. It flew out.

The Masticate

In the days, waiting, every move
in the house led to the clerestory
window, where a nest turned its insides
to me. In an orbit of sticks, shredded
bits, in a clutch of pink rhododendrons,
in the mouths of newborn robins
cracked from their tombs, their beaks
always open to eat, my mother returns
from the dead as the mother bird
masticates worms, crickets, a livery
of small creatures dug from the earth.
All day I watched. All day I chewed
on this verb; it seemed all stressed
syllables as my lover chopped carrots
and onions in the kitchen, as a cat
curled her claws in the bark of a tree.

Wraith

Unnaturally, the small brown bird
with the striated breast
under the park bench is not anyone I know,
just a wren, mute and pecking
at something under the gray leaves
under the ivy. She doesn't remind me
of anyone, though I try to consider her as,
first, one lost friend, then another.
My mother, who is dead, is always a cardinal,
a bird she craved seeing, but one
who stayed away, for fear of the cat.
Today, tired, I try out a dream technique,
and still no one comes. Perhaps,
tired of my complaints, no one
will inhabit anything other than
what they are: the dead remain dead,
disappointed friends stay disappointed, the ones
who love me love me, god knows why.

Office Sonnet

To Ted on the other side of my cube:
I'm sorry your mother does not
remember you called her ten minutes ago,
and I'm sorry you have to move her
from her home, the one you grew up in.

And even though we have never spoken
about anything but the weather and
spikes in the news, I'm sorry you have no
privacy, and I'm sorry you have to listen
to me schmooze with my lover, long distance,

and honk business on the phone
every day. I hope your retirement plans
work out, though no one is supposed
to know. Your secrets are safe with me.

Village Butcher

I consider the sun scorching the sidewalk
where I live, where I exact
a living wage of pleasure
each morning. Whether I want to or not,
I get up. I judge my life the way
the butcher, two blocks away,
gauges the weight of prime rib
in his shop, precisely, without measure,
as he does this morning
slicing fat, dressing the slab
as if prime rib were an ode he is writing
to food. He examines his life
between slices. Conscious.
Alone. He's outlived his father,
his mother. He inherits the store.
He answers the phone
and wipes blood from his glove—
while I wait—glad to be loved
by someone he clearly loves back.
He stands, knife in hand,
and considers her voice, the chords
as they climb through her mouth,
then his, then mine.

Catch

The whole gamut of our immigrant
love pools here, in what each of us
grasped before meeting. We traveled so light
our sacks were superfluous, hoboes, tramps,
rail riders of the certain now,
more complex than electricity,
plainer than the noses on our faces:
Irish, Russian, granddaughters of bakers,
butchers from Pittsburgh, Philadelphia.
On this boat to America, we think we invented
the self, this new species, the body, its net.

II.

Tidings

In the channel two fishermen
cast for false albacore
chasing a meal,

their congress like news
best read from inside
the oncoming tide. From inside

a dozen tiny nicks stung
my skin. I touched a green slick
the length of an eye-

lash caught in the rub
of my suit,
one soft shell in a bloom of crabs,

thousands born by a swirl-
ing current. My lesson:
learning to swim

a distance. Small live bits
knocked into my arms, down
my chest, over my legs.

All summer I lived
in my body. Completely.
Relying on matter,

not language,
I read these tiny
bodies, moving,

inexact. All summer
I studied how humble
the body is

breathing. No classical
strokes, no tracing a dip
of my head curling

under the arc of my arm.
All summer my instruction
eschewed

convention. I learned to submit
my body
to space,

to the cycle of plankton
and progeny, to ferry
myself among others, to commute.

Sailing

After learning their sea name and deployment,
all day I watched the telltales attached
to the sail, red slips of fabric gauging
the wind, the boat itself
a new encounter, the captain
and her first mate strangers to me,
except they knew my surname
and a few scraps, the kind of material
that unfolds over cocktails and green swells.

The wind pressed an acceptable twelve knots,
so we swiftly came about an island
and cove whose names lent themselves
to metaphor. I stopped testing my acuity
for calm. This vacancy occupied hours.
The cut of sun and clouds referenced
the depth of pleasure, how long it lasts, and how
contentment drains you, you,
not moving a limb—in any direction.

Causeway

Outside your idea of me
I stray. I keep to myself
as much as anyone can
keep to herself
beside you. You, sniffing,
like a rat catcher,
like a terrier that is friendly
until it catches some
thing run amuck.

Walking the causeway,
I'm invisible, stirred
under the radar
of your thinking,
where I snag and catch myself
wanting to be
somewhere else,
not here, where
the marsh and bay
divide at our sides.

Here I hide like a dog,
like the rat catcher I am.

Below, scratching the sand,
even the tiniest crustacean
finds a place other than her skin
to retreat to. The hermit crab,
squeezed in a shell,

contorts her own body
to carry the weight
of a hard-won
scholarship on her back.

First Person

In the rearview mirror an egret
lifts off from swamp grass;

in the driveway you wave me away.
I leave the original way, in person.

But you, remembered, are sharper,
more beautiful in the poem, carried

this way, the way a playwright
might feature your gestures

in the act of the heart breaking
over and over so the sound of the heart

breaking is sharper and more
beautiful than the original heartbreak,

so nearly unbearable you'd never
wish to feel it, directly, again.

Tincture of Happiness

You,
with your long legs,
the juice of fresh basil
crushed between thumb
and forefinger,
fragrant after a swim,
sea salt in your hair.
The grass, cut by you,
the late ferry,
met by you,
the stick of summer
drawn out of moist air
by your breeze.
And
the mourning doves
not really
mourning at all.
Nothing to grieve
all day—
the day, still whole,
without a puzzle,
without a fracture,
with only
you
to foment.

To Summer

I'll admit I looked forward to your departure,
the end of the heat wave, the black spit
of mulberry, the last of our best goblets
dashed. Right now you are speeding, leaving
the north road, shedding the threaded vineyards,
the herb and goat farms, each numbered exit
closing the gap between you and your syllabus,
our school year apart. Mack Trucks race, freighted
like you with obligations. Already, I wish
it were May and you, with your good reasons
for quitting the job, stood in the yard, your bike
still bolted to its rack. I wish we were now
pulling on our suits. You, with your long legs,
your never-veering attention to my faults.
Maybe my virtues will swim to the surface when you,
with your open-to-be-thwarted heart, come back.

Instinct

She lifted a wizened head above
the surface, a thin stump
joined by others: terrapin turtles,
pregnant, straining their necks
toward the shore. Each year each
goes back to the bank
of her birth. Such swimming
trust in the earth. I dipped a paddle
into the brackish salt water.
They dove, spotting me.
Not leaving, not joining,
I passed among them
as I passed you, yards away,
in another craft.

Swimming the Sound

And with each stroke the water
wedged itself into our bodies,
and with each stroke the sea grass
shivered as we drew near

the shore. And with
each stroke your face
became smaller and your strong
arms disappeared, needle thin

in the light as it mellowed
and hollowed the space
between us. What should have been
all that dreaming

under the glassy surface
only left things glassy on the surface.
And all that dreaming under
the shimmering, dwindling

light on the Sound left us
shimmering, dwindling.

A Psalm Sung by a Fish

Heady is the current that carries us
without exertion,
undetected,

the absence of refuse. Sublime,
the trapless bay,
the boatless harbor,

the green-gray waves
cresting overhead.
Auspicious, the airtight oil tanker,

the honorable sea captain,
the righteous longshoreman
standing watch

over the docks. Humble
are those who navigate
this spring migration. The fish

hawk scans the shore, circles back.
Surely she sees us. Lucky
for the flash that teased her

to pass—if I had a knee
I'd bend it in thanks. Fish
are not known to believe,

but I might be
persuaded,
living this long,

traveling this far
on the earth
in the sea.

Recovered Blue

Speck of a shell
no bigger than

an acorn nib
attached to my skin

after a swim, a sliver
from a mollusk's

lodge, bluer
than any painted blue,

deepest when wet,
hollowed by salt.

Splinter, sorrow,
a structure from which

even the sea
has been taken.

Sea School

Given the earth is (merely) 29% land
it's no wonder we boat
on planks of wood and fiberglass—
giddy visitors, suspended over
the dominant culture of sea,
of ocean: bodies of water
named and unnamed.

And *no wonder,* I say this—
seated in an office: *no wonder . . .*

* * *

Scene from my desk:

water towers,

poured cement window bays,

copper-greened patina of parapets,

the open mouths of drains.

* * *

On a nautical wall chart:

the land, beige; the sea, white.
My step penetrates a surface—

the mind in the body drifts
without touching ground,
maybe for days.

***

Modes of access:

color codes, catalogued mysteries
transport us
if only over the Hudson.

And by this I mean
the mind carries us
over the river itself.

The body: 71% water.

Where in the world is this?

***

My hand glides underwater,
my hair, my pores,
a taut envelope.

Crushed sea grasses
rest like palms for the holy crossing
of body to thought.

A bridge may be the closest
we get to the murk,
the salt majesty,

the everyday workplace
of a deck hand, sea captain.

***

Certification:

every tide I give myself over to,
every estuary,
every studied and unstudied
submersion. Submission.

III.

Monoprint of a Shoe

Tongue, heel, sole,
laces and eyelets, oh shoe
on a flatbed, dissected,
these parts are not
the sum of your whole

life, the grass and the gravel,
the snow, the mud we've met.
The soot that collects
in your cracks is
age, polished, the scent

made soft, your body
misused, laid
under a bed, dumped
in a closet. Oh valued
companion, now finished,

accessory to crimes,
the commitment of living:
to the graveside,
to the wedding, to work,
to the station.

You are the conditions
taking me. You fit my step.

Deciding to Walk

Because I couldn't find the subway
right away, because the night air
was the softest it's been
in a year,

suddenly lonely, without a plan
and no friend to call, and
wanting to feel this
clearly,

last night I decided to walk
home forty blocks
past tourists making
memorial signage,

past the post-disaster
cleanup into
after-work chatter wafting

from darkened bars
into the stink of junkie
pharmaceutical waste

on cracked pavement.
I could have chosen the *new* New York,
listing along the Hudson,
her kayak armada,

her encouraging bike paths,
azaleas, evergreened landfill.

I could have let my spirits be lifted,
but I wanted to taste the city

where little remains
undocumented,
the grit left out of these plans
for the new world order.

Collage

After the opening, after
the toasts and first courses,
after the strands of our past
lives meet & unravel,
we discover we *are*
the middle-aged strangers
from New Jersey
who join us, torn
from another century,
names changed, accents lost,
new ones acquired in the boroughs,
in Manhattan, artists
and working class, heroes,
clerks and collector
tycoons. These small-buttoned
landscapes—a grid, a map
pecked out in ticket stubs,
coat checks, pins and needles
pointing, warning labels,
pulled from their pillows—become a collage
of benign signs. Even in these
toxic times, we live, we thrive.

Splitting the House for Art

—in praise of Gordon Matta-Clark

You cracked open the curious corridors,
cut through the kitchen, still standing
outdoors, drew a blade to the portico,
sliced sunlight through the roof.
A lucky strike.
The ground heaved, joined by a crane
and her cronies. Here you are:
gathered in a gable, suspended in chains.

Taken

This is the boat that took me
out of my marriage,
the painter said, then clicked

to the next slide. Here is the chair,
the spare table I pulled my grief
up to. Here is where the gash

of oil paint put me: behind
a door closed, thick green
strokes refusing to leave.

Estate Sale

Everything must go. Not much
is left. Jesus on the wall

in her study, over her bed,
on the cross, on the lampshade,

on His knees at the window,
His expression is plastic,

pastel. Neighbors whisper
in French down the hall.

Saint Peter & His Fish
50 cents on the porch.

Saint Christopher plucked
from the trash. Mary,

pulled from the rose garden,
leans on Saint Francis

in a wheelbarrow, their robes
covered by leaves. Jesus,

silent, with friends
at the table, hours

before His death,
framed under her unlit

candelabra. Strangers
pick through her stemware,

her Tupperware. A family friend
shrugs at an offer, makes change.

In a closet, Jesus swings
from her beads, glows in the dark.

April

Spring is the undug grave,
what this late blizzard
spells, renting sidewalks
and a wrought iron fence.

At the corner Our Lady
of Perpetual Sorrow crouches,
guarding her church. Everyone else
darts under awnings,

brushing coats and hair.
A traffic cop gestures in vain.
Winter is closer and meaner
than you think. My mother

knew this of course, those final days,
her blood urging her heart to stop squalling.

Death of an Iowa Farmer

We stared at the farmer laid out
in an open casket, her face
blue, a shade even the undertaker
had never seen and could not
quell. Blue as the light blue veins
in her wrists, blue as the faint sky
falling over the tractor that trapped her
body, her soul already pressed into pigment.

Heaven

When my sister lifted the World War II
Army-green flight suit
from a bag, our dead mother,

as WAC, stepped into her empty
pant legs, returned to us
quiet as dust. We carried her up

from the basement. Mice, nesting
in waves of wrinkled wool, left
teeth marks in fabric. Her wartime

wedding band's vines
curled in my palm with an old rosary
blessed by Pope Pius VI

for my mother, a pregnant
believer, in Rome.
Still, I refuse to pray

on dead wood. Some days,
I confess, I caress a circle
of painted orange beads

with a coconut cross I bought
in a zócalo market. Sometimes
I find them to finger

in secret, walking home
from work in Manhattan. Once
I found them in a winter coat pocket

on a plane as the workers de-
iced the wings. You might call this
a prayer, a return to that moment,

that year I believed God
lived in Mexico's mountains.
Trees rushed the sky

as the sky, itself,
gathered thousands of migrating
monarchs. I saw them lift off,

saw the shape of my body, leaving
my body, on a ridge. My body
as air. Not one I'd known,

or had ever known. Not one
I'd seen, or had ever seen
before this.

Knife & Fork

I haunt the old Seafood Barge, safe
in the neck of the harbor, as though I were
already its ghost, run out of town,
as if this were years from now, and new
wealth finally outweighed the thrift
of the locals. The menu's peppered
with fresh ginger, no more lobster
in the rough. And the better-educated
girls take the places old hags held—
waiting on tables, sucking their teeth,
their syntax salty and foul. I smooth
the plain white paper on its way to be
linen. I twist a knife, now plastic,
soon to be silverware, shiny, then dull.

Class

I lasted three days minding a child
at the beach club on a thin strand
of sand, where my family lived
but did not belong. I took over the job

my sisters had before me,
my sisters, who sat every summer,
gladly, reading books, getting tans,
earning money for college.

On the second day I knelt by the pool,
the north Atlantic in sight,
the Isles of Shoals clearly raised
in the distance. I watched a girl

not much younger than I swimming
laps. The sun bleached the water
in the pool, licking its sides
the way my soft drink

licked my glass. Idle, like the idle rich
parents at the bar, I watched this girl
as if reading would be stealing
the attention they paid for. This was

my lesson. Back and forth she swam,
back and forth I weighed belonging
and not belonging, the salt water,
always free, the steps to it already mine.

IV.

Borrowed House

Never will I own this view, though
your neighbor all week has attempted to

fence his in. The ferryboat lobs its way
north, then south, then north, then south,

and the pair of osprey arrived
from who knows where, back again, hungry

and ravaging one another in
a mating ritual you'll see every spring

now that you live here too. I draw this view,
a gentle *lap lap lap*, from your house,

the wind as it topples a sunfish and drags
the Wednesday flotilla across the bay and back,

the way we push and pull one another
as we buffet the past, as I see it, through glass.

Summer Commerce

A boy mows the strip of grass
between a Boston Whaler for sale
on the lawn next to
a row of granite headstones,
cut to show how they'll look
on new graves. Some are still smooth
and for now unnamed.

Desire

I long for their dark, half-ton
bodies shambling, dark
fur in the dark curb
of the wood. Is this shade
under the summer maple
one of them? Is this smudge
on a shrub a cub? Nothing to see.

A friend sends this image
from Dover, New Hampshire,
from her turn-of-the-century farm-
house, close to town, close
to heaven flushed out of hiding.

Word spread from Durham
to Lee, from Madbury
to Newmarket: bird feeders tossed,
the scrape of long nails scored
the boards of a deck;
on the ten o'clock news, one
finger points to nothing
as haunting as all I can't see.

The Horse in Her

for Maxine Kumin

The horse in her led us into the wood,
crossing paddock and fence, over creek
and fallen oak, where the stark sun leaked
between branches more and more barren
with every gust of wind. The weeping leaves,
prescient and thick as they filled the hollows,
fell faster and faster as they stuffed
every place we looked down to for balance.
Steady at 80, she led us, shifting
her legs over a thick trunk
blocking the path, intent on finding
the mushroom grove a mile deeper in.
Their white heads, as she predicted,
peered from a lunar bed freckling the sweep
of pine needles, orange, between roots
of rotted trees. The soft space invited her
to fold and roll her body down, knowing
if one horse rolls the others follow.

Caryatid

Bent, for choosing the Persians over
the Greeks, her neck and crown
hold up the roof's flat cornerstone,
the history of architecture
in her gesture. She must hoist her bad
choices through time. I stand
weighing her progress. How to
measure her fate, carved to shape
an example of her? She
carries her strong nature in her robes
so like a pillar, an elegy, her poem.

Pollyanna Redux

My spin turns loss
into asset

and twists in the maker
who casts me

alone with the evil aunt
in the attic room,

who makes me
glad to get crutches

for Christmas, glad
not to need them.

I had to lose
my mother, my father,

otherwise there'd be no
silver lining, no cliché

to make bearable
the everyday obscene.

I'd like a word with the author.
I'd like to tell her: grow up!

I'd like to tell her:
today

I plan to be unforgiving.
I plan to be inconsolable,

just once. I plan to stop
reinventing the father,

the substitute mother.
I recruit my old friends

in fiction. Orphans, originals:
Heidi rethinks her trek

up the Alps. Snow White
reclines in a slump.

I call Cinderella,
who places Prince Charming

on a shelf. We unearth
the sour, the bitter, the selfish,

our collective
unuttered umbrage.

Together, we stew the past
and make a boil out of it.

What He Carried

A stale breeze bore the news,
dropping it with a specificity
we could taste. A substance
we couldn't identify
twisted up from the sidewalks
gathered on street signs
and lights. Early that day, a co-
worker's brother pitched down
eighty-six stories, tramped
forty-four blocks north,
rode our faulty office elevators
eight floors up to wait
for his brother, who wasn't here.
Black and blue, cinder-lidded
he waited, then left,
walked to Broadway,
mute with what he carried
in his hair, his eyes, his mouth.

Magnolias

You reach, thick and flush, over sidewalks
to inhabit the air, Brooklyn, spring
before summer suckles the breeze
out of it. Your arms, a former lover's,
classic and damaged, a South America
that could have been Paris, but isn't:
civilized, democratic, but never new
like the New World suggests. Each day
a steamship of possibility. All I see
is the blue in your magenta, your pitted
sorrow, your South, waiting to wake,
a pulse, dim, but still there, blue
lines under your thick shell.

"Lake Camp"

I regret
I did not buy

your small
looked-over landscape.

Thick paint
now occupies

that part of the brain
I retreat to—

the small boat,
a black stroke after sunset;

your pines, foothills,
the lake itself—

brown shades
at this hour.

Only the frame
is darker.

I inhabit the sliver
of light—left on—

in the cabin:
bone white.

Hook & Line

Now that we've agreed
to be spontaneous
together, I picked a cove

for its benevolent bow,
late spring, the perfect
time to simply be

on the beach, just us, before
the summer crowds
step off the ferries,

reflecting the Sound's salt
surface. Here the stones
are smooth, white and ochre.

Some, green, stained
by dried sea, still cling to
debris, curious,

sometimes embarrassing.
Paired differently now,
we let our new partners unpack

the napkins, the glassware.
A rusted fishhook catches
my rug as I spread it, and you

pull at the nylon line,
still attached, to protect me.

After You

At the time I thought I was dying
I finished what I started.
I accomplished a lot. Nothing strayed
from the list, every *i* dotted.

Days refused to drag, so full, besotted.
My skin tingled. Sun stroked it.
I dropped extra pounds, walked
everywhere. I ran, really, the rush of arrival

heady and grim. Now that I know I will live,
mail goes unanswered. The phone rings.
I let it. My nails grow jagged, unkempt.
Appointments stray: doctors, the dentist, hair.

What's the hurry, now that time
stretches and bends?

Notes

"Collage" is for Michael Cooper

"Death of an Iowa Farmer" is for Curtis Bauer

"Desire" is for Mary Jo Gauthier

In "Estuary English" the author owes a debt to the "vernacular investigations" of John R. Stilgoe and his Shallow-Water Dictionary: A Grounding in Estuary English

"Monoprint of a Shoe" is for John Kramer

"Onion Field" is written in memory of Jorge Voorduin

"Splitting the House for Art" is in praise of the work of Gordon Matta-Clark

"The Horse in Her" is for Maxine Kumin

"Tidings" is for Ellen Neff

Acknowledgments

The author wishes to express her grateful acknowledgment to the editors and publishers of the following publications in which these poems, some in earlier versions, first appeared:

American Poetry Review: "Denizen," "Monoprint of a Shoe," "Turnstile," "A Bird in the House," "Night. Fire," "Desire"

Barrow Street: "Magnolias"

Bellevue Literary Review: "Tidings"

Bloom: "Death of an Iowa Farmer," "To Summer"

Global City Review: "Deciding to Walk," "First Person," "Office Sonnet," "Swimming the Sound"

Hawaii Pacific Review: "Catch"

Hubbub: "After You," "Village Butcher" (as "Knots")

Mantis: A Journal of Poetry, Criticism, and Translation: "Splitting the House for Art"

The Massachusetts Review: "Recovered Blue," "Taken"

Mid-American Review: "Wraith"

New Letters: "The Horse in Her"

Poetry: "Lower Manhattan Pantoum"

Rattapallax: "Estate Sale"

River Styx: "Onion Field"

Upstreet: "What He Carried"

The Women's Review of Books: "Class," "The Masticate"

(continued)

Special thanks to the following sites for reprinting these poems
online: "Lower Manhattan Pantoum," on Poetry Daily
(www.poems.com); "Lower Manhattan Pantoum," "Night. Fire," and
"Onion Field," on From the Fishouse (www.fishouse.org)

The band Tarwater used "Lower Manhattan Pantoum" as text in a
musical composition on their album *Spider Smile*, Morr Music, Berlin,
Germany, 2006.

For assistance in the preparation of this manuscript, I thank Curtis
Bauer, Theresa Burns, Teddy Laurel, Martin Mitchell, Tom Mohan, and
Jeet Thayil.

photo by Joyce Culver

Elaine Sexton is the author of *Sleuth*, a collection of poems by
New Issues Press (Western Michigan University) in 2003. Her poems,
reviews, essays, and art criticism have appeared in *American Poetry
Review*, *ARTnews*, *Art New England*, *Prairie Schooner*, *Poetry*, *River
Styx*, *New Letters*, *the Writer's Chronicle (AWP)*, and numerous other
journals. She teaches a poetry workshop at the Writing Institute at
Sarah Lawrence College, works in magazine publishing, and lives
in New York City.

New Issues Poetry

Vito Aiuto, *Self-Portrait as Jerry Quarry*
James Armstrong, *Monument in a Summer Hat*
Claire Bateman, *Clumsy, Leap*
Sandra Beasley, *Theories of Falling*
Kevin Boyle, *A Home for Wayward Girls*
Jason Bredle, *Standing in Line for the Beast*
Michael Burkard, *Pennsylvania Collection Agency*
Christopher Bursk, *Ovid at Fifteen*
Anthony Butts, *Fifth Season, Little Low Heaven*
Kevin Cantwell, *Something Black in the Green Part of Your Eye*
Gladys Cardiff, *A Bare Unpainted Table*
Kevin Clark, *In the Evening of No Warning*
Cynie Cory, *American Girl*
Peter Covino, *Cut Off the Ears of Winter*
James D'Agostino, *Nude with Anything*
Jim Daniels, *Night with Drive-By Shooting Stars*
Joseph Featherstone, *Brace's Cove*
Lisa Fishman, *The Deep Heart's Core Is a Suitcase*
Noah Eli Gordon, *A Fiddle Pulled from the Throat of a Sparrow*
Robert Grunst, *The Smallest Bird in North America*
Paul Guest, *The Resurrection of the Body and the Ruin of the World*
Robert Haight, *Emergences and Spinner Falls*
Mark Halperin, *Time as Distance*
Myronn Hardy, *Approaching the Center; The Headless Saints*
Brian Henry, *Graft*
Edward Haworth Hoeppner, *Rain Through High Windows*
Cynthia Hogue, *Flux*
Joan Houlihan, *The Mending Worm*
Christine Hume, *Alaskaphrenia*
Josie Kearns, *New Numbers*
David Keplinger, *The Clearing; The Prayers of Others*
Maurice Kilwein Guevara, *Autobiography of So-and-So:
        Poems in Prose*
Ruth Ellen Kocher, *When the Moon Knows You're Wandering;
        One Girl Babylon*
Gerry LaFemina, *The Window Facing Winter*
Steve Langan, *Freezing*
Lance Larsen, *Erasable Walls*

David Dodd Lee, *Abrupt Rural; Downsides of Fish Culture*
M.L. Liebler, *The Moon a Box*
Alexander Long, *Vigil*
Deanne Lundin, *The Ginseng Hunter's Notebook*
Barbara Maloutas, *In a Combination of Practices*
Joy Manesiotis, *They Sing to Her Bones*
Sarah Mangold, *Household Mechanics*
Gail Martin, *The Hourglass Heart*
David Marlatt, *A Hog Slaughtering Woman*
Louise Mathias, *Lark Apprentice*
Gretchen Mattox, *Buddha Box, Goodnight Architecture*
Carrie McGath, *Small Murders*
Paula McLain, *Less of Her; Stumble, Gorgeous*
Lydia Melvin, *South of Here*
Sarah Messer, *Bandit Letters*
Wayne Miller, *Only the Senses Sleep*
Malena Mörling, *Ocean Avenue*
Julie Moulds, *The Woman with a Cubed Head*
Carsten René Nielsen, *The World Cut Out with Crooked Scissors*
Marsha de la O, *Black Hope*
C. Mikal Oness, *Water Becomes Bone*
Bradley Paul, *The Obvious*
Jennifer Perrine, *The Body Is No Machine*
Katie Peterson, *This One Tree*
Jon Pineda, *The Translator's Diary*
Elizabeth Powell, *The Republic of Self*
Margaret Rabb, *Granite Dives*
Rebecca Reynolds, *Daughter of the Hangnail; The Bovine Two-Step*
Martha Rhodes, *Perfect Disappearance*
Beth Roberts, *Brief Moral History in Blue*
John Rybicki, *Traveling at High Speeds* (expanded second edition)
Mary Ann Samyn, *Inside the Yellow Dress; Purr*
Ever Saskya, *The Porch is a Journey Different From the House*
Mark Scott, *Tactile Values*
Hugh Seidman, *Somebody Stand Up and Sing*
Heather Sellers, *The Boys I Borrow*
Martha Serpas, *Côte Blanche*
Diane Seuss-Brakeman, *It Blows You Hollow*
Elaine Sexton, *Sleuth; Causeway*
Marc Sheehan, *Greatest Hits*
Heidi Lynn Staples, *Guess Can Gallop*
Phillip Sterling, *Mutual Shores*
Angela Sorby, *Distance Learning*
Matthew Thorburn, *Subject to Change*